PAPER

Gareth Stevens Publishing
A WORLD ALMANAC EDUCATION GROUP COMPANY

Please visit our web site at: www.garethstevens.com
For a free color catalog describing Gareth Stevens Publishing's
list of high-quality books and multimedia programs,
call 1-800-542-2595 (USA) or 1-800-387-3178 (Canada).
Gareth Stevens Publishing's fax: (414) 332-3567.

Library of Congress Cataloging-in-Publication Data

Paper.
     p. cm. — (Let's create!)
   Summary: Step-by-step instructions show how to use different kinds of paper,
such as poster board, crepe paper, and napkins to create original craft projects.
   Includes bibliographical references.
   ISBN 0-8368-3747-9 (lib. bdg.)
   1. Paper work—Juvenile literature. [1. Paper work. 2. Handicraft.] I. Series.
TT870.P353   2003
745.54—dc21   2003045405

This North American edition first published in 2003 by
Gareth Stevens Publishing
A World Almanac Education Group Company
330 West Olive Street, Suite 100
Milwaukee, WI 53212 USA

First published as *¡Vamos a crear! Papel* with an original copyright © 2001 by
Parramón Ediciones, S.A., – World Rights, text and illustrations by Parramón's
Editorial Team. This U.S. edition copyright © 2004 by Gareth Stevens, Inc.
Additional end matter copyright © 2004 by Gareth Stevens, Inc.

English Translation: Colleen Coffey
Gareth Stevens Series Editor: Dorothy L. Gibbs
Gareth Stevens Designer: Katherine A. Goedheer

Printed in Spain

1 2 3 4 5 6 7 8 9 07 06 05 04 03

Table of Contents

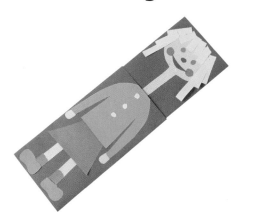

Introduction

Most paper is made from a mixture of plant fibers and is sold in thin sheets, but different kinds of paper are made for different purposes. Some kinds of paper are made especially for drawing. Paper called stationery is made for writing. Waxed paper and cellophane are made for wrapping food. Tissue paper is made to be very soft, so it is the best kind of paper for napkins, paper towels, and toilet paper.

The kinds of paper you will need for the projects in this book can all be used for the same purpose — to create crafts. This book contains twelve simple crafts made with paper, including a handy booklet with a collage on the cover, a colorful clown doll, a curvy cat, and some fabulous flowers. All of the projects are meant to be a starting point for inventing your own paper creations.

Because paper is a material that is used so often and for so many purposes, finding it at home or at school should be very easy. To work with paper, you need only scissors, a glue stick, tape, and a few other simple, easy-to-find supplies.

The kinds of paper you will use range from simple white sheets to aluminum foil and include thin tissue paper, thick construction paper, stretchy crepe paper, and crinkly cellophane. Some projects call for poster board in particular colors. If you have white poster board, however, you can color it yourself with crayons, colored pencils, or paints.

Watch for special instructions at the end of each project to try other great ideas. Sometimes, making just one small change creates a very different result.

Start creating craft surprises with paper of all kinds and sizes!

Collage-Covered Booklet

Making an apple collage is as easy as pie and adds an artistic flair to this useful little accordion-style booklet.

You will need:
- scissors
- 8.5- x 11-inch (21.5- x 28-cm) sheets of paper in many different colors
- ruler
- colored marker
- glue stick

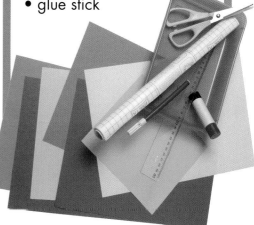

1 Cut a piece of paper so it measures 4 x 4 inches (10 x 10 centimeters) and draw an apple on it with a colored marker.

2 Cut many small scraps out of different colored sheets of paper.

3 Glue paper scraps that are shades of blue around the outside of the apple to make a background. Glue scraps in shades of red inside the apple. Make a leaf out of green paper and glue it onto the apple.

4 Fold 4 sheets of paper in half, lengthwise. Each sheet of paper should be a different color. Cut along the folds to make strips.

5 Fold the strips into 4- x 4-inch (10- x 10-cm) squares that have a small flap on one side. Alternating colors, glue together the folded strips to look like an accordion.

6 Glue the apple collage onto the front of the accordion.

This colorful booklet is the perfect place to keep your friends' telephone numbers.

Another Great Idea!
Instead of gluing the pages of the booklet together, make a hole in one corner of each square and hold the squares together with a brass paper fastener.

Carnival Hat

Tissue paper polka dots and paper garland fringe can turn a plain party hat into a flashy carnival decoration.

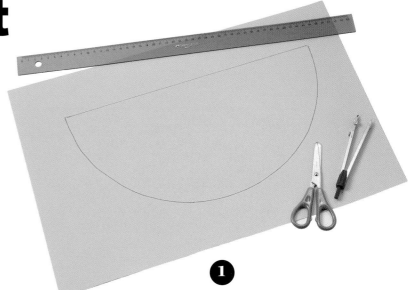

1 Use a compass and a ruler to draw a large half circle on a piece of yellow poster board. Cut out the half circle and roll it into the shape of a cone. Glue it together so it looks like an ice cream cone.

2 Cut out circles of pink, green, and orange tissue paper. You can make a lot of circles at one time by folding a piece of tissue paper many times, then cutting one circle through all the folded layers.

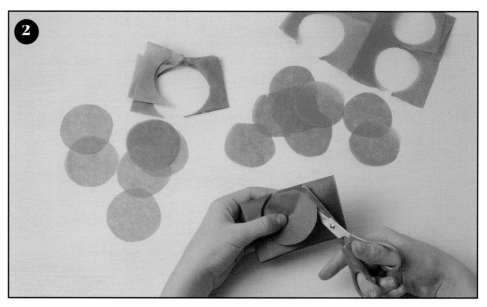

You will need:
- compass
- ruler
- yellow poster board
- scissors
- glue stick
- pink, green, and orange tissue paper
- latex glue
- paintbrush
- yellow paper garland

3 Mix latex glue with a little water. Brush glue onto the tissue paper circles, one at a time, and stick each circle onto the yellow cone.

8

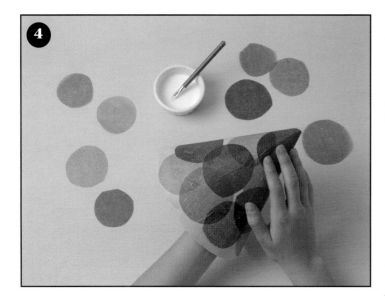

4 As you glue on more circles, overlap them until they cover the outside of the cone.

5 Use a glue stick to attach yellow garland around the edge of the cone. Also, glue a small piece of garland to the point of the cone.

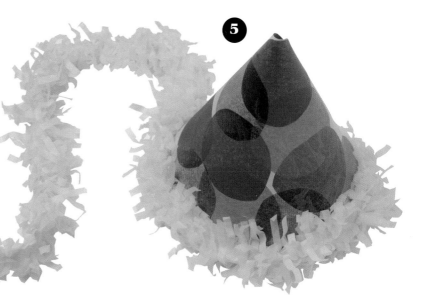

This hat is festive enough for any party. You could even wear it in a parade.

Another Great Idea!
For a different look, glue on the tissue paper in vertical stripes or in other shapes.

Calico Clown

This cute clown is dressed for the circus, but with a piece of blue string attached to his head, he's happy to hang around with you instead!

You will need:
- thin, pointed, wooden stick
- small paper ball
- paintbrush
- white, red, blue, and tan paints
- scissors
- multicolored paper garland
- yarn needle
- blue string
- orange paper garland
- glue stick
- red crepe paper

1 To make the clown's head, push the point of a thin wooden stick into a small paper ball. Brush tan paint all over the paper ball and let it dry. Paint eyes, a nose, and a mouth on the ball with white, red, and blue paints.

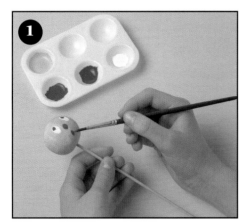

2 Cut two pieces of multi-colored garland. Make one of the pieces longer than the other. Tie the pieces of garland together at the centers with blue string. The shorter piece will be the arms. The longer piece will be the legs.

3 Use a yarn needle to poke a hole through the clown's head. Thread the blue string through the hole to attach the head and the body.

4 Cut a small piece of orange paper garland and glue it to the top of the clown's head, for hair.

5 Cut a strip of red crepe paper and wrap it around the clown's body like a belt. Glue down the end of the crepe paper to hold it in place.

Wrap his string around your finger to make this clever clown dance.

Another Great Idea!
Make the paper ball for the clown's head out of newspaper mixed with white glue and water (papier mâché) or by wrinkling up tissue paper with a small amount of latex glue.

11

Curly-Q Cat

This comical cat starts with a curl. Then all you have to do is add a cute face and a curvy tail.

You will need:
- ruler
- green poster board
- scissors
- black and white colored pencils
- glue stick

1 Measure a strip of green poster board 2 inches (5 cm) wide and cut it out.

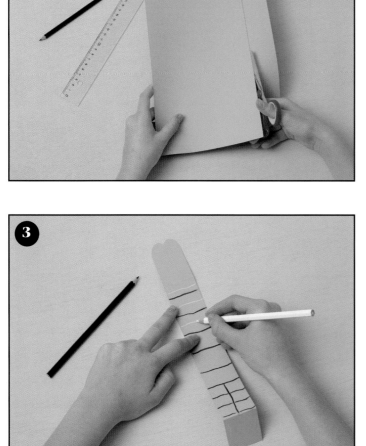

2 Fold the strip at 2 inches (5 cm) on one end and at 3 inches (7.5 cm) on the other end. Cut the short edge of the longer folded end into two rounded paws.

3 Draw black and white horizontal stripes from one fold to the other. Draw a vertical black line (as shown) to make legs.

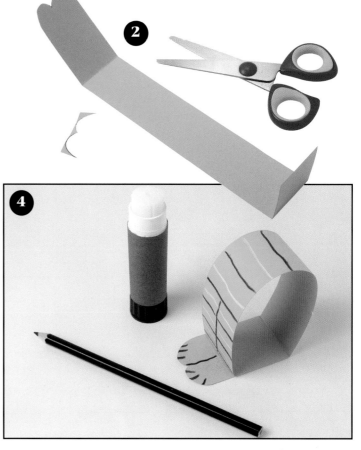

4 Curl the strip around and glue the end down 2 inches (5 cm) behind the paws. Draw black claws and a line between the paws.

5 On the leftover piece of green poster board, draw the head and face of a cat and a long, curvy tail with black and white stripes on it. Cut out the head and the tail.

Now, isn't this curly kitty the cat's meow?

6 Glue the cat's head above the feet on the front of the curled body. Use scissors to make a slit on the back of the body, then push the cat's tail through the slit.

Another Great Idea!
Use smaller strips of poster board, in different colors, to make kittens.

Small-Town Scenery

Set the stage for playtime with a town you build yourself out of cardboard and cutouts. It's easy!

You will need:
- blue, green, and red poster board
- glue stick
- scissors
- colored markers
- yellow, blue, and brown wrapping paper
- sheet of white paper
- ruler
- square and rectangular colored stickers
- red tissue paper
- aluminum foil

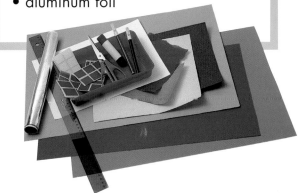

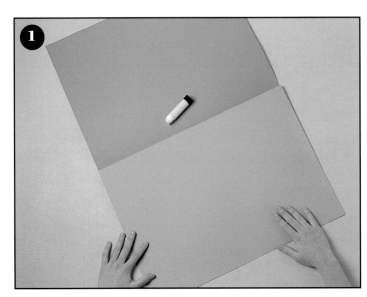

1 Cover the bottom half of a piece of blue poster board with green poster board and glue the green poster board in place.

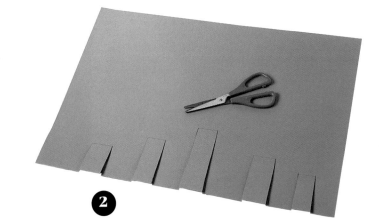

2 Fold the upper half of the blue poster board down over the green poster board to make a type of folder. Cut ten slits, at different distances apart, along the folded edge to make five fringes in the crease of the folder.

3 Draw a sun on yellow wrapping paper and two clouds on a sheet of white paper, then cut them out. With the folder open, glue the sun and the clouds to the blue poster board, which will be the sky.

4 Draw the shapes of two large houses and two small houses on red poster board and cut them out.

5 Glue on yellow wrapping paper to cover the lower part of each small house. Glue on blue wrapping paper to cover the lower part of one large house, then glue brown paper on the other large house. Leave the roofs of all four houses uncovered.

6 Use square and rectangular stickers of different colors and sizes to put doors and windows on all of the houses.

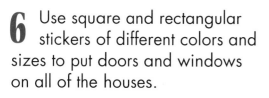

15

7 Draw the shape of a tree on green poster board and cut it out. Glue on brown wrapping paper to cover the trunk.

8 Make little balls out of red tissue paper and glue them on the treetop to look like fruit.

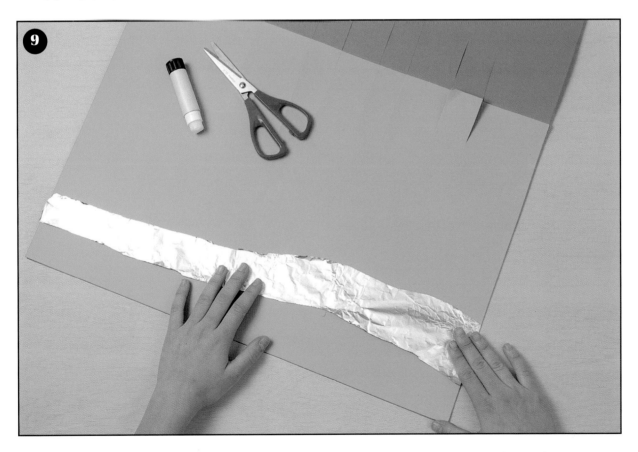

9 Cut a strip of aluminum foil and glue it across the green poster board to make a river. The green poster board will be grass-covered land.

10 Bend the sky forward at the crease, to stand upright, with the fringes folding toward you. Glue the houses and the tree to the fringes, attaching one object to each fringe.

You have just constructed a small town! Make up some stories about it, then use your town as scenery to tell them.

Another Great Idea!
Construct a city with skyscrapers, or a mountain scene, or a farm with animals.

Frilly Flower

Colored crepe paper makes fabulous flowers! When you see how easy it is, you'll want to make a bunch.

1 Cut pink, red, and purple crepe paper into short, wide strips. Cut three strips of each color, then fold each strip in half.

2 Take one folded strip of each color to make a group of petals and attach it, with transparent tape, to one end of a thin wooden stick. Repeat this step two more times.

You will need:
- scissors
- pink, red, and purple crepe paper
- transparent tape
- thin wooden stick
- green tissue paper
- glue stick

3 Cut a long strip of green tissue paper.

4 Put glue on the strip and wrap it, first, around the bottom of the petals, then, down the entire stick.

5 Carefully open the folded crepe paper to make the petals of the flower blossom.

Combining many different colors of crepe paper will give you an endless variety of flowers.

Another Great Idea!
Make a bouquet of different colored flowers with different stem lengths. Wrap the bouquet in a large piece of tissue paper.

Growing Girl

How would you like to make a paper doll that can actually grow? Impossible, you say? Not when you follow these instructions!

You will need:
- long sheets of pink paper
- black marker
- blue, red, yellow, orange, green, white, and tan paper
- scissors
- glue stick

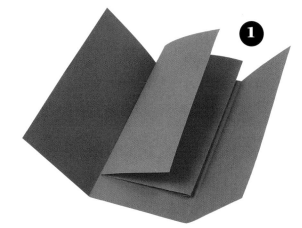

1 Fold two long sheets of pink paper into three sections. One sheet should be folded a little smaller than the other, so it will fit inside the larger folded sheet.

2 Draw a head with a long neck on a piece of tan paper. Cut it out and glue it to the outside panel of the pink paper that is folded smaller.

3 Use colored paper to make blue eyes, a red nose and mouth, yellow hair, and orange cheeks. Cut them all out and glue them onto the head.

4 Using more colored paper, make green shoes and a green shirt, white buttons, an orange skirt, blue socks, and tan legs and hands.

5 Cut out all the colored parts and glue them, in the correct body positions, onto the outside panel of the larger folded pink paper.

6 Insert the head panel into the body panel so it will slide in and out.

Now do you see how this paper doll grows?

Another Great Idea!
Fold three sheets of paper and glue the doll's legs and feet onto a third panel. This paper doll will grow at both the neck and the legs!

Crafty Carryall

Carrying books and toys around will be easier, and more fun, in this delightfully decorated bag.

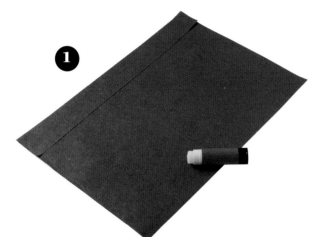

You will need:
- scissors
- blue, yellow, and brown wrapping paper
- glue stick
- colored markers
- green circle stickers

1 Cut a piece of blue wrapping paper 16 x 28 inches (40 x 70 cm). Make a 4-inch (10-cm) flap on one long side. Fold one short side over 12 inches (30 cm), then fold the other short side over it. Tuck one side of the top flap under the other, then glue the sides together.

2 To make the bottom of the bag, fold the corners at the end of the paper without the flap 2 inches (5 cm) inward. Then, fold that end up, making another flap, and glue it down.

3 To make handles, cut two strips of blue wrapping paper. Fold each strip in half, lengthwise, then fold both ends of each strip forward, forming a U. Glue the ends of the handles to the inside edge at the top of the bag. Put one handle on each side.

4 Draw the shape of a giraffe on a piece of yellow wrapping paper and cut it out.

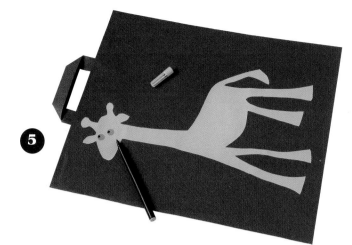

5 Glue the giraffe onto the bag. Put green circle stickers on its face for eyes and draw pupils on the stickers with a black marker.

6 On brown wrapping paper, draw four hooves, a tail, two nostrils, a patch of hair, and small spots of different sizes. Cut out each part and glue it in place on the giraffe's body.

You're done! You can use this colorful carryall as a gift bag, too.

Another Great Idea! Decorate bags with other animals you like or with pretty flowers.

Day 'n' Night Dazzler

You can turn day into night!
Surprise your friends with this
magical work of art.

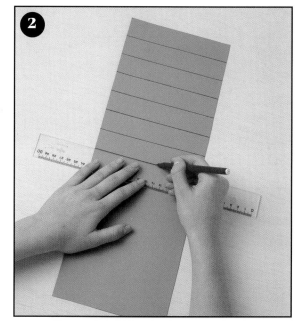

1 Divide a sheet of white paper in half. On
one half, draw a moon and stars (night).
On the other half, draw a sun and clouds (day).

2 Cut a piece of blue poster board
6 x 16.5 inches (15 x 42 cm) and
draw lines across it, dividing it into
fourteen 1¼-inch (3-cm) sections.

You will need:
- 8.5- x 11-inch (21.5- x 28-cm)
  sheet of white paper
- colored pencils
- scissors
- blue poster board
- ruler
- colored marker
- glue stick

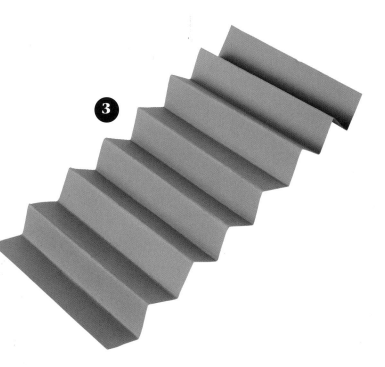

3 Fold the poster board along each line,
alternating the direction of the folds to
make them look like an accordion.

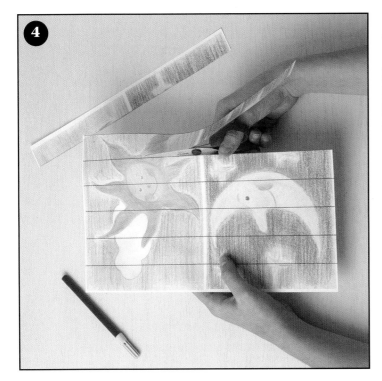

4 Divide each drawing into seven 1¼-inch (3-cm) strips, then cut the strips apart.

5 Glue the strips onto the folds in the blue poster board, alternating the strips, one at a time, from each drawing, in the correct order.

From now on, day and night will depend on which direction you're looking from.

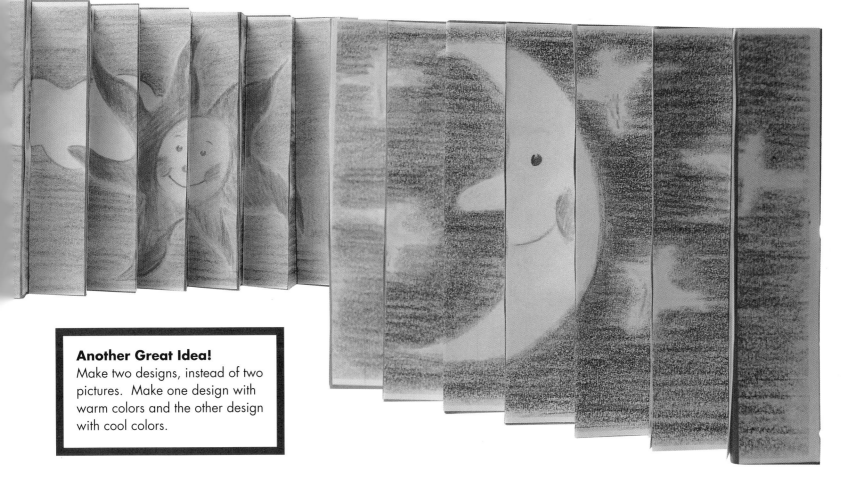

Another Great Idea!
Make two designs, instead of two pictures. Make one design with warm colors and the other design with cool colors.

Roly-Poly Puppet

Turn a cardboard tube into a clever toy. All it takes is colored paper, glue, and imagination.

1 Cut strips of pink, blue, orange, and purple paper. Make each strip a different width.

You will need:

- scissors
- pink, blue, orange, purple, and green sheets of paper
- glue stick
- cardboard tube from a roll of toilet paper
- black marker
- small green and red circle stickers
- large white circle stickers

2 Cut a narrow strip of green paper, then make triangular cuts along one side. Cut a wider strip of green paper and make small slits in one side, all the way across, to form fringe.

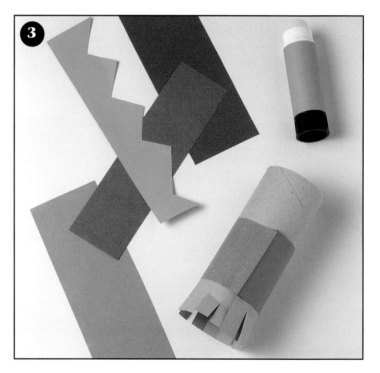

3 Glue the strip of fringe around one end of a cardboard toilet paper tube. Then glue on the orange, purple, blue, and pink strips, overlapping them. Glue the green strip with the triangular edge on last, around the bottom.

4 To make eyes, draw a big black dot, for the pupil, inside each of two green circle stickers.

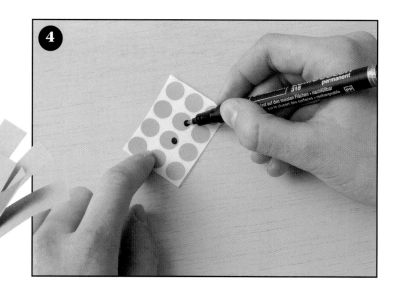

5 Using the orange strip for a face, put a red circle sticker (nose) in the center. Put a white sticker on each side of the red one, but slightly higher. Finally, put a green eye on each white circle.

Put your hand inside the tube to make this toy a puppet.

Another Great Idea!
Combine different colors or add more stickers to make many different puppets. Use them as napkin holders, too.

Tricky Telephone

At last, you can have your own phone! You just have to make one. With these instructions, you can make a telephone that looks almost real. It might even fool your friends.

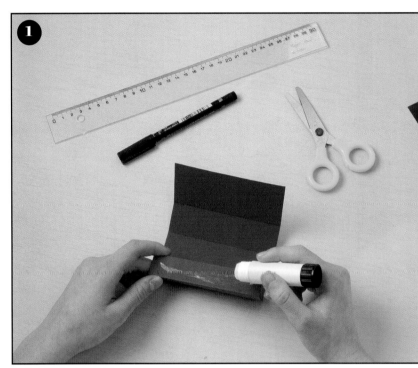

1 Cut a piece of red poster board 4.5 x 7 inches (11 x 18 cm). Draw lines 2, 3, 5, and 6.5 inches (5, 8, 13, and 16 cm) from one short edge. Fold the poster board on each line. Glue the small flap left over at the end to the opposite edge to form a box.

2 Attach a white rectangular sticker at one end of one of the wide sides of the box. This sticker will be the screen.

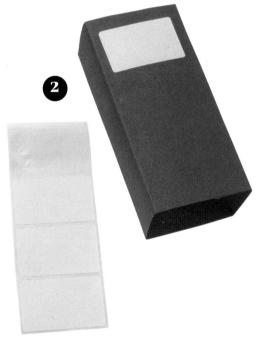

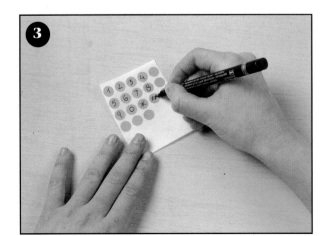

3 Use a black marker to draw numbers (0 to 9), an asterisk (*), and a pound sign (#) on green circle stickers. Draw one number or symbol on each sticker.

28

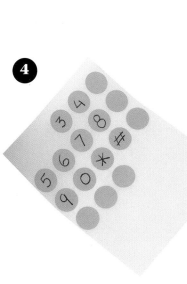

4 Stick the circles numbered 1 through 9 onto the phone, under the screen, in three rows. Make a fourth row with the *, the 0, and the # stickers.

5 With a white pencil, draw an antenna on black poster board and cut it out. Glue the antenna to the top of the telephone.

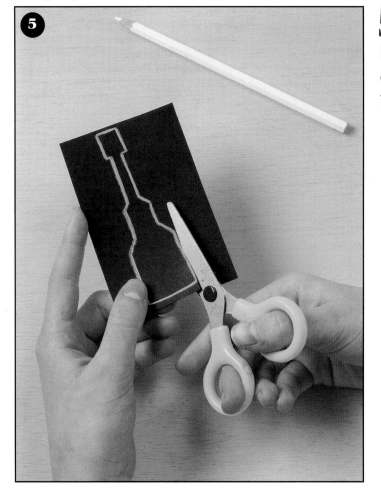

Another Great Idea!
Make other accessories to add to your telephone or write numbers or a message on its screen.

Riiiing! Riiiing! Time to take your first call on this tricky telephone.

Candy Dandy

Crinkly cellophane makes a fun-size piece of candy. Striped paper stockings make this candy a dandy!

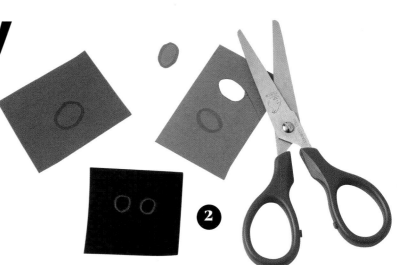

1 Roll up a yellow paper napkin, then wrap it in a piece of yellow cellophane. Twist the ends of the cellophane to make it look like a big piece of hard candy.

2 Draw one circle on red poster board (nose), two circles on blue poster board (eyes), and two smaller circles on black poster board (pupils for the eyes). Cut out all of the circles.

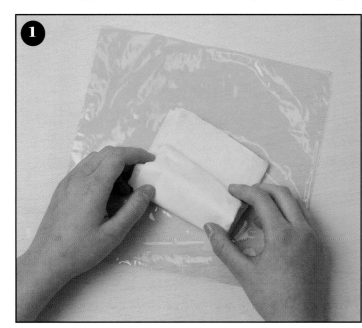

3 Glue the eyes and the nose to the center of the cellophane candy to make a face.

You will need:
- yellow paper napkin
- yellow cellophane
- colored marker
- red, blue, black, yellow, and green poster board
- scissors
- glue stick
- transparent tape

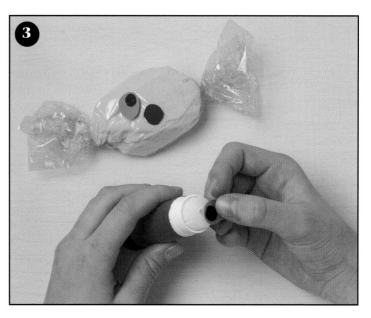

4 Draw two legs and feet on yellow poster board and cut them out.

5 Cut small strips of red, blue, and green poster board and glue them onto the legs to make stripes.

6 Use transparent tape to attach the tops of the legs to the back of the cellophane candy.

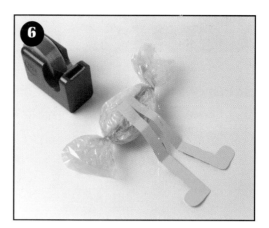

Now you have a nifty party decoration. You can also use this long-legged dandy instead of a bow to wrap a gift.

Another Great Idea!
Paint different artistic designs on separate pieces of cellophane. After the paint is dry, wrap a folded napkin in each piece of cellophane to make decorative "hard candies."

Glossary

accessories: items or objects that add to the beauty or effect of a main object

alternating: arranging something in a repeating pattern

calico: marked with small patterns or with blotches of many different colors

carryall: a bag or a carrying case that can hold many items

cellophane: strong, transparent paper with a smooth, filmlike surface

collage: art work that has small pieces of colored images and materials arranged in a design and attached to a background

dandy: (n) a man who dresses stylishly

flair: a special look or quality that makes something more attractive

fringes: hanging threads or thin strips of material that form a decorative border

garland: a ropelike wreath made of decorative materials

panel: a flat, rectangular piece of material that is a distinct part of a larger surface

shades: the same color appearing lighter and darker

transparent: clear; see-through

More Books to Read

10 Minute Activities: Paper. Andrea Pinnington (VHPS Virginia)

Cardboard Tube Mania. Christine M. Irvin (Children's Press)

Let's Start Collage. Emma Foa (Silver Dolphin)

Little Hands Paper Plate Crafts. Laura Check (Williamson)

Paperfolding. Clive Stevens (Heinemann Library)

Pop-o-mania: How to Create Your Own Pop-ups. Barbara Valenta (Dial Books)

Web Sites

A Paper Palace. www.familyfun.go.com/ crafts/season/feature/famf87project/ famf87project15.html

Paper University Art Class: Recycled Paper Beads. www.tappi.org/paperu/art_class/ paperBeads.htm